Staying Connected While Social Distancing

by Grace Hansen

THE CORONAVIRUS

Abdo Kids Jumbo is an Imprint of Abdo Kids
abdobooks.com

abdobooks.com

Published by Abdo Kids, a division of ABDO, P.O. Box 398166, Minneapolis, Minnesota 55439.
Copyright © 2021 by Abdo Consulting Group, Inc. International copyrights reserved in all countries.
No part of this book may be reproduced in any form without written permission from the publisher.
Abdo Kids Jumbo™ is a trademark and logo of Abdo Kids.

Printed in the United States of America, North Mankato, Minnesota.

052020

092020

THIS BOOK CONTAINS
RECYCLED MATERIALS

Photo Credits: AP Images, iStock, Shutterstock, ©Shutterstock PREMIER p.11

Production Contributors: Teddy Borth, Jennie Forsberg, Grace Hansen
Design Contributors: Dorothy Toth, Pakou Moua

Library of Congress Control Number: 2020936731
Publisher's Cataloging-in-Publication Data

Names: Hansen, Grace, author.

Title: Staying connected while social distancing / by Grace Hansen

Description: Minneapolis, Minnesota : Abdo Kids, 2021 | Series: The Coronavirus | Includes online
    resources and index.

Identifiers: ISBN 9781098205539 (lib. bdg.) | ISBN 9781098205676 (ebook) | ISBN 9781098205744
    (Read-to-Me ebook)

Subjects: LCSH: Social distance--Juvenile literature. | Interpersonal relations--Juvenile literature. | Social
    media--Juvenile literature. | Videoconferencing--Juvenile literature. | Emotional health--Juvenile
    literature. | Epidemics--Juvenile literature.

Classification: DDC 302.2310--dc23

Table of Contents

COVID-19

When **COVID-19** spread to the US, many new terms were being used. One term was "**social distancing**." Another was "flattening the curve." These two things are related.

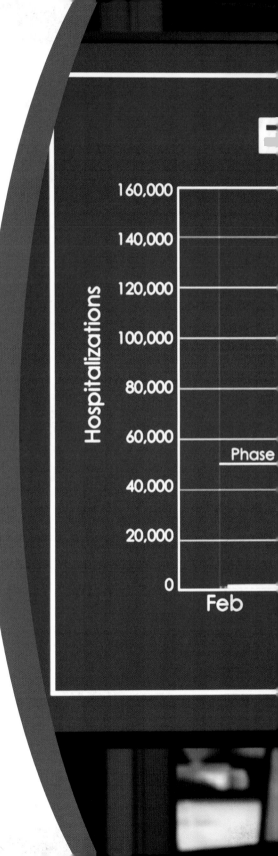

COVID-19 is an illness caused by a new **coronavirus**. People did not have any **immunity** to the virus. It spread very easily. This is why **social distancing** was important.

Flattening the Curve

Social distancing keeps people apart. This makes it harder for the virus to spread. That is because the virus mainly spreads from person to person.

When the virus doesn't spread quickly, we flatten the curve! The curve is **steep** if lots of people get sick at the same time. The curve flattens if the number of sick people is spread out over time.

key

curve without
social distancing

curve with
social distancing

hospitalizations

hospital limit

date

11

Staying Connected

Social distancing is important. But it can cause us to feel lonely. We cannot see our friends or family in person. We might miss special events, like birthdays and holidays.

It is good to feel connected.
There are lots of ways to
connect! One way is to set up
weekly video chats with people.
Then you have something to
look forward to each week.

Taking a break from technology can be nice. Ask a friend or family member to be your pen pal. Take turns writing letters to each other. These letters are sent through the mail.

Some older people live in nursing homes. **Social distancing** can be extra hard on them. You could draw nice pictures with happy messages. Ask an adult to find an address to send it to.

Chalk pictures and messages are also fun! You can draw pretty things on sidewalks. It will make your neighbors smile!

21

More Information About COVID-19

- **COVID-19** is short for <u>Co</u>rona<u>v</u>irus <u>D</u>isease 20<u>19</u>.

- COVID-19 is an illness caused by a coronavirus strain called SARS-CoV-2.

- SARS-CoV-2 is short for severe acute respiratory syndrome coronavirus 2.

- Common symptoms of COVID-19 include cough, fever, and shortness of breath.

Glossary

coronavirus – one in a group of viruses that cause disease. In humans, coronaviruses cause respiratory tract infections, like a common cold or a more deadly illness.

COVID-19 – short for Coronavirus Disease 2019, the illness caused by a new strain of coronavirus. Common symptoms include fever, cough, and shortness of breath. More serious symptoms can occur in some people.

immunity – the ability to resist a certain virus by the action of certain antibodies.

social distancing – the practice of keeping a greater than usual physical distance (such as 6 feet or more) from other people, or avoiding direct contact with people and objects in public places during the outbreak of a contagious disease.

steep – having a sharp slope or slant.

Index

Abdo Kids
ONLINE
FREE! ONLINE MULTIMEDIA RESOURCES

Visit **abdokids.com**
to access crafts, games,
videos, and more!

Use Abdo Kids code
TSK5539
or scan this QR code!